WHAT
IS
MEDITATION?

WHAT IS MEDITATION?

J. KRISHNAMURTI

Edited by Duncan Toms

RIDER

1

Rider, an imprint of Ebury Publishing
20 Vauxhall Bridge Road
London SW1V 2SA

Rider is part of the Penguin Random House group of companies
whose addresses can be found at global.penguinrandomhouse.com

Penguin
Random House
UK

Compiled by Jerome Blanche
kfoundation.org

J. Krishnamurti has asserted his right to be identified as the author of this
Work in accordance with the Copyright, Designs and Patents Act 1988

First published by Rider in 2023

www.penguin.co.uk

A CIP catalogue record for this book is available from the British Library

ISBN 9781846047541

Typeset in 11.5/15 pt Bembo Book MT Pro by Jouve (UK), Milton Keynes
Printed and bound in Great Britain by Clays Ltd, Elcograf S.p.A.

The authorised representative in the EEA by Penguin Random House
Ireland, Morrison Chambers, 32 Nassau Street, Dublin D02 YH68

Penguin Random House is committed to a sustainable future
for our business, our readers and our planet. This book is made
from Forest Stewardship Council® certified paper.

INTRODUCTION

Meditation is a central theme of Krishnamurti's talks and writings. Seeing the growing popularity of meditation and the myriad of techniques and approaches on offer, Krishnamurti eschewed the practices, goals and controls advocated by teachers and traditions. Meditation, he says, is not something you do or even experience, nor can it be learned from another. Therefore, this is not another book explaining *how* to meditate.

What, then, is meditation? The quotes and extracts presented here, each a meditation in itself, unfold Krishnamurti's unique approach to a subject both astonishingly simple and with great depth. He suggests meditation is directly related to our everyday activities, not something separate, and is only possible with order in our daily life. Meditation is not forcing the mind to be quiet, nor concentration or contemplation; it is a profound awareness of the nature of self and thinking, with the possibility of thought finding its right place – a revolutionary freedom from the known:

Meditation is a movement in attention. Attention has no border, no frontier to cross; attention is clarity, clear of all thought. Thought can never make for clarity, for thought has its roots in the dead past; thinking is an action in the dark. Awareness of this is to be attentive. Awareness is not a method that leads to attention; such attention is within the field of thought and can be controlled or modified; being aware of this inattention is attention. Meditation is not an intellectual process; it is freedom from thought and a movement in the ecstasy of truth.

J. Krishnamurti is considered one of the greatest philosophers and teachers of all time. His work has influenced major figures such as George Bernard Shaw, David Bohm, Alan Watts, Henry Miller, Bruce Lee, Eckhart Tolle, Jackson Pollock and Aldous Huxley.

What Is Meditation?

Learning about oneself, whatever one is, is the beginning of meditation. When you are learning, there is no accumulation. The moment you have acquired, gathered, it becomes knowledge, and what you call learning adds more to what you already know. What you already know conditions your learning. So learning is never accumulation.

There is no meditation if there is no self-knowing. There is no meditation if there is no right foundation. The laying of the right foundation is meditation. Laying the foundation is to be free from ambition, from envy and greed, from the worship of success. That is, there is the beginning of meditation with self-knowing. Without self-knowing, there is no meditation – whatever you call meditation is self-deception or self-hypnosis, with no meaning whatsoever. The methods and systems people offer, how to meditate, are all so utterly immature. We are talking of meditation based on the right foundation. If you go very far after laying the foundation, which is self-inquiry and self-understanding, deep down, there is no challenge and no response. That is a long journey, not in time, not in days and years, but a journey that has to be taken ruthlessly within oneself.

Meditation is to understand the whole movement of the known and to see whether it is possible to move away from it.

If I am aware that I am neurotic, I am already coming out of that neuroticism. But most of us are not aware of our peculiarities and slightly unbalanced states, our exaggerations, idiosyncrasies and fixations. To be aware of this neurotic condition requires attention, watching, but we have not the energy, time or inclination to observe ourselves; we would rather go to an analyst or somebody who will do the job for us and complicate our life even more. If you are aware that you are neurotic – not only superficially but deeply, as most of us are – then to bring about a change, you must be aware, you must watch every word, what you feel and think, go into yourself profoundly. Perhaps then, out of that awareness, comes meditation.

Investigating the ending of sorrow is part of meditation – not the escape into visions.

Self-knowledge is the beginning of meditation. Without knowing yourself, repeating words from the sacred books has no meaning at all. They pacify, quieten your mind, but you can do that with a pill. By repeating a phrase over and over and over again, your brain naturally becomes quiet, sleepy and dull. In that dullness and insensitivity, you might have experiences, get certain results, but you are still ambitious, envious, greedy and creating enmity.

Meditation is the understanding of the self. Without this understanding, what is called meditation, however pleasurable or painful, is merely a form of self-hypnosis. You have practised self-control, mastered thought and concentrated on furthering experience, which is a self-centred occupation, not meditation. To perceive that this is not meditation is the beginning of meditation. To see the truth in the false sets the mind free from the false. Freedom from the false does not come about through the desire to achieve; it comes when the mind is no longer concerned with success or the attainment of an end. There must be the cessation of all search, and only then is there a possibility of the nameless coming into being.

Self-deception exists when there is any form of craving or attachment: attachment to prejudice, an experience or a system of thought. Consciously or unconsciously, the experiencer is always seeking greater, deeper, wider experience. As long as the experiencer exists, there must be delusion in one form or another.

Time and patience are necessary for the achievement of a goal. An ambitious person, worldly or otherwise, needs time to gain an end. The mind is the product of time, and all thought is its result. Thought working to free itself from time only strengthens its enslavement to time. Time exists only when there is a psychological gap between what is and what should be, the ideal, the end. To be aware of the falseness of this whole manner of thinking is to be free from it – which does not demand any effort or practise. Understanding is immediate; it is not of time.

When the false has dropped away, there is freedom for that which is not false to come into being. You cannot seek the true through the false; the false is not a steppingstone to the true. The false must cease wholly, not in comparison to the true. There is no comparison between the false and the true; violence and love cannot be compared. Violence must cease for love to be. The cessation of violence is not a matter of time. The perception of the false as the false is the ending of the false.

Let the mind be empty and not filled with the things of the mind. Then there is only meditation and not a meditator who is meditating.

In meditation, you must understand the significance of thought, its value and its total irrelevancy in going beyond measurement.

In meditation, don't follow anybody, including myself. Don't follow any system because it will make your mind dull and destroy whatever energy you have. You need tremendous energy to go beyond all thought.

Our minds are trained to accept and conform. Our thoughts are shaped according to somebody else. We have become imitative, conformist and incapable of freedom to observe for ourselves. Therefore the mind has to re-educate itself in understanding why it, and the whole of our being, accepts conformity.

Why do you conform? Why do you accept the pattern set by another, about meditation or anything? We accept what the doctor says, the engineer, the architect, the scientist and so on, because they have specific knowledge. But the guru, leader or teacher, the one who tells you how to meditate, what do they know? Please inquire into it: what do they know? Knowledge is always in the past.

If you are deeply interested in this question of meditation – the movement of meditation, the act of meditation, to discover what it means – we have to look at the question of authority. What form of meditation and how to meditate is a question of authority. But where there is authority, there can be no freedom, neither in the tyrannical world of dictatorship and totalitarian states, nor in meditation.

The word *authority* means one who originates something (as in the word *author*), and people follow, make what they say into an authority and then it is dead. This is especially true here because if you follow what I say, it is finished. You must be very careful, if you want to go into this question of meditation, to be completely, wholly, inwardly free from all authority and comparison. I don't know if you can do it.

Therefore you must be extremely aware of the importance of authority in one direction – of the doctor or scientist – and understand the total unimportance of authority inwardly, whether it is the authority of another, which is fairly easy to throw off, or the authority of your own experience, knowledge and conclusions, which becomes prejudice. You must be equally free from the authority of another and your own authority.

The first thing to realise in meditation is that there is no authority, that the mind must be completely free to examine, to observe, to learn.

Meditation is the denial, the negation of all systems because you see the truth and understand the full significance that you must be your own light. This light cannot be the light of another, nor come through another, and you cannot light that light from another. If you once see the truth of this, you will not follow a single human being – no guru, no saviour, no priest with their doctrines, traditions and rituals. This is going to be awfully difficult because we are afraid to stand alone.

Authority and following another, whether a system, a method or a practice, have no place in meditation.

Meditation is the discovery, the attention that brings order in your life, and therefore in society.

Is it possible for the mind to end conflict? – all conflict, not only conscious but deep down, the hidden layers that have never been exposed, which may be the cause of conflict. I cannot end conflict without knowing the whole content of myself – the will, the escapes, the desires, the demands, the sexual urges, all the twists, perversions and tortures I am in.

Now, does the mind learn all this content gradually or instantly? If it is a gradual process, you will die without learning it all. If it is a gradual process, it involves time – many days, years or just a few minutes. In that time, all kinds of pressures and distortions are going on. Time is not the way to understand it, and there must be a different way. Can I learn about myself – which is a very serious thing, in which there is no deception at all – completely in the instant?

Now meditate. Meditate now. After all, meditation is sharpening the mind. No book, no relationship, no argument is ever going to produce that quality of sharpness. You offer me that, and you say, 'It is your food, cook it,' and I have to find out. There is no cookbook, no chef, no leader – I have to find out. Which means I have to use every form of ingenuity.

Meditation is bringing about order in life and thereby gathering great energy. Meditation is ending conflict between the observer and the observed, which adds further energy.

Real meditation is not possible if I don't understand conflict. I see that conflict distorts, is a poison, a neurotic state to be in. I see that; that is the truth. To me, that is an absolute truth, as fire burns. Now I say to myself: How am I to be free of conflict without creating another conflict? In trying to be free of conflict, there is another. I don't want to do that because it prolongs the conflict. I have to find a way of ending conflict without introducing others.

If you meditate without order, you are living in a series of fantasies, in imagination, in romantic illusion.

In the non-attentive state is conflict. Observe that conflict, be aware of it, give your total attention to that conflict so that the mind becomes extraordinarily alive and non-mechanical. That is part of meditation.

There is no controlling or disciplining thought in meditation because the one who disciplines thought is a fragment of thought.

When there is control, there is direction. Direction and control imply will. In the desire to control, a goal and direction are established, which means carrying out a decision made by will. The carrying out is the duration of time. Therefore a direction means time, will and an end – all this is implied in the word *control*. What place has will in meditation, and therefore in life? Or has it no place at all, meaning there is no place for decision – only seeing, doing, which doesn't demand will or direction.

Meditation in daily life is action in which there is neither choice nor will.

Meditation is necessary for the mind to be completely still. When the mind is completely still, it is in total order: there is not a single movement of wasting energy. That silence, that quietness, that complete tranquillity of the mind is not something put together by thought.

You have been trying to bring about silence, quietness, peace of mind, and in that is control. You are trying to control thought, which is wandering all over the place – a segment of that thought tries to control the movements of other thoughts. In this control, you have never inquired into who the controller is. Who is the controller and the thing controlled? Do look at it. The controller is one of the fragments of thought which has broken itself up into different fragments.

Then you sit quietly and want to meditate. What you call meditation, not what we are talking about. You sit quietly, and your thought wanders off. The controller brings thought back and tries to say, 'Don't go away.

Remain. Be concentrated.' Another thought comes up, and you think about something else, and again this battle goes on. You call this meditation, but it is a total waste of energy. Can the mind be free from all control? Give your heart to this, find out.

Any form of control denies sensitivity and intelligence, which are demanded in meditation.

What is meditation? In considering meditation, effort and the maker of effort must be understood. Good effort leads to one thing and bad effort to another, but both are binding. It is this bondage that must be understood and broken.

Meditation is the breaking of all bondage. It is a state of freedom, but not *from* anything. Freedom *from* something is the cultivation of resistance. To be conscious of being free is not freedom. That consciousness is the experiencer, the maker of effort. Meditation is the breaking down of the experiencer, which cannot be done consciously. If the experiencer is broken down consciously, there is a strengthening of the will, which is also a part of consciousness. Our problem, then, is concerned with the whole process of consciousness and not with one part of it, small or great, dominant or subservient.

We call the unraveller of consciousness the higher self, the *atman* and so on, but it is still part of

consciousness: the maker of effort who is everlast-
ingly trying to get somewhere. Effort is desire. One
desire can be overcome by a greater desire, and that
desire by still another and so on, endlessly. Desire
breeds deception, illusion, contradiction and visions
of hope. The all-conquering desire for the ultimate,
or the will to reach that which is nameless, is still the
way of consciousness, of the experiencer of good
and bad, the experiencer who is waiting, watching,
hoping. Consciousness is not of one particular level;
it is the totality of our being.

The mind is an instrument that has been put together. It is the fabric of time, and it can only think in terms of results, of something to be gained or avoided. The mind is ever seeking a result, a way to some achievement.

As long as the mind is active, choosing, seeking, experiencing, there must be the maker of effort who creates an image. This is the net in which thought is caught. Thought itself is the maker of the net; thought *is* the net. Thought is binding; thought can only lead to the vast expanse of time, the field in which knowledge, action and virtue have importance. However refined or simplified, thinking cannot break down thought. Consciousness as will, the experiencer, the observer, the chooser, the censor, must come to an end, voluntarily and happily, without any hope of reward. The seeker ceases. This is meditation.

Silence of the mind cannot be brought about through the action of will; there is silence when will ceases. This is meditation. Reality cannot be sought; it *is* when the seeker is not. Mind is time, and thought cannot uncover the measureless.

There is security in total intelligence. That intelligence is not yours or mine; it is intelligence. In that security, the brain cells become quiet.

There is intelligence when the mind is capable of observing that which is false, and because it has seen the false, there is security. The mind becomes extraordinarily quiet naturally, easily, sweetly, without any effort, and in that stillness there is no time. It is not a question of whether the mind can sustain that silence – that is the desire of thought, wanting to pursue silence as pleasure. In that silence, there is no experiencer, no observer, but only that quality of complete and total silence. In that silence, the door is open. What lies beyond the door is indescribable; it cannot be put into words. All that you can do is come to the door and open it. It is your responsibility as a human being.

The whole of this is meditation: the absolute quietness of the body, the absolute quietness of a totally religious mind, in which there is no spark of violence or conflict. Violence exists where there is will. When you have understood all this, when you have lived this in daily life, you come to that door, and you open it and discover. Open that door.

In total silence there is nothing. You are nothing. If you are something, there is no silence. When there is noise, you cannot hear or see. Only when the mind is nothing is there complete security, complete stability. Only then can the mind find out if there is, or if there is not, something that is nameless, something that is beyond time. All this is meditation.

You have to live a daily life in which relationship with another has no conflict. All this is meditation. It is only then you come upon that which is timeless. If you don't know how to have relationship without conflict, life becomes distorted, ugly, painful, unreal. Relationship is life.

Meditation is to have a completely still mind. It can only be still naturally – not a cultivated stillness, not a practised stillness. If you practise stillness, it is a death and is no longer stillness.

Silence cannot come through practice or control. Silence is not between two noises; it is not the peace between two wars. Silence comes when the body and mind are in complete harmony, without any friction. In that silence, there is a total movement which is the end of time. Time has come to an end.

There is much more to meditation: to find that which is most sacred. Not the sacredness of the idols in temples, churches or mosques – those are man-made, hand-made, made by the mind, by thought. There is a sacredness not touched by thought. That can only come about, naturally, easily, happily, when we have brought about complete order in our daily life. When there is such order, which means no conflict, out of that comes love, compassion and clarity. Meditation is all this, not an escape from daily life. Those who know the quality of this meditation are blessed.

The brain has its own rhythm, but that rhythm has been distorted by extravagance, by ill-treating the brain through drugs, through faith, through belief, drinking and smoking. All that has distorted the brain, and it has lost its pristine vitality.

Meditation is the sense of total comprehension of the whole of life, and from that comes right action. Meditation is the absolute silence of the mind, not a relative silence or the silence that thought has projected and structured. It is the silence of order, which is freedom. Only in that total, complete, unadulterated silence is truth, which is everlasting from everlasting. This is meditation.

Meditation without a set formula, without a cause or reason, without end or purpose, is an incredible phenomenon. It is not only a great explosion that purifies; it is also death. It has no tomorrow. Its purity devastates, leaving no hidden corner where thought can lurk in its own dark shadows. Its purity is vulnerable; it is not a virtue brought into being through resistance. It is pure like love because it has no resistance.

There is no tomorrow in meditation, no argument with death. The death of yesterday and tomorrow does not leave the petty present of time (and time is always petty). Meditation is destruction to false security. It is new. Meditation is not the silly calculations of a brain in search of security.

There is great beauty in meditation, not the beauty of things that have been put together by humanity or by nature, but of silence. This silence is emptiness in which, and from which, all things flow and have their being. It is unknowable: neither intellect nor feeling can make their way to it. There is no way to it, and a method to it is the invention of greed.

The ways and means of the calculating self must be destroyed wholly. All going forwards or backwards, which is the way of time, must come to an end, without a tomorrow. Meditation is destruction; it is a danger to those who wish to lead a superficial life of fancy and myth.

A man was sitting cross-legged in a remote corner of the park, his bicycle beside him. He had closed his eyes, and his lips were moving. He was there for more than half an hour in that position, completely lost to the world, to the passers-by and to the screech of parrots. His body was quite still. In his hands was a rosary covered by a piece of cloth. His fingers were the only movement one could see, apart from his lips.

He came there daily towards the evening, and it must have been after his day's work. He was rather a poor man but fairly well-fed, and he always came to that corner and lost himself. If you asked him, he would tell you he was meditating, repeating a prayer or mantra — and to him that was good enough. He found in it solace from the everyday monotony of life.

He was alone on the grass and behind him was flowering jasmine. A great many flowers were on the ground, and the beauty of the moment lay around him. But he never saw that beauty, for he was lost in a beauty of his own making.

Meditation is not the repetition of words, the experiencing of a vision or the cultivation of silence. The bead and the word do quieten the chattering mind, but this is a form of self-hypnosis. Meditation is not wrapping yourself in a pattern of thought or the enchantment of pleasure. Meditation has no beginning, and therefore it has no end.

If you say, 'I'll control my thoughts, sit quietly in a meditative posture and breathe regularly,' you are caught in the tricks with which one deceives oneself. Meditation is not a matter of being absorbed in a grandiose idea or image: that only quietens one for the moment, as a child absorbed by a toy is for the time being quiet. As soon as the toy ceases to be of interest, the restlessness and the mischief begin again. Meditation is not the pursuit of an invisible path leading to imagined bliss.

The meditative mind is seeing, watching, listening, without the word, without comment, without opinion.

It is attentive to the movement of life in all its relation-
ships throughout the day. At night, when the whole
organism is at rest, the meditative mind has no dreams,
for it has been awake all day. Only the indolent have
dreams; only the half-asleep who need the intimation of
their own states. But as the mind watches, listens to the
movement of life, the outer and the inner, to such a
mind comes a silence not put together by thought.

It is not a silence the observer can experience. If you
do experience it and recognise it, it is no longer silence.
The silence of the meditative mind is not within the bor-
ders of recognition, for this silence has no frontier. There
is only silence in which the space of division ceases.

Can the mind be absolutely still? That which is still has great energy. It is the summation of energy.

Meditation demands tremendous attention. Where there is attention, there is great energy.

Meditation is total attention to whatever you are doing throughout the day. If you are putting on your tie, attend to it. If you are talking to somebody, pay complete attention. In attention, there is no centre as the 'me'. Only when there is no attention is there the formation and structure of the self, from which all sorrow, pain and division arise.

Meditation is this sense of total absence of the self. When there is that attention, the mind becomes completely quiet, silent, without any pressure. This silence is not the invention of thought; it is the complete quietness of the mind. And that which is silent has vast space. Thought has no place in space. Only then does that which is nameless come into being. Then life, all life, yours and another's, all existence becomes sacred, holy. This is the meaning of life and the meaning of meditation.

The word *meditation* is very loaded. In Asia, it has been given a particular meaning. There are different schools of meditation, different methods and systems aiming to produce attention. Some systems teach meditation as control, or follow an idea, or look at a picture and live with that image endlessly, or take a phrase and go into it, or watch the movement of your big toe, or listen to a word, Om or Amen, and follow the sound, or repeat Sanskrit phrases – and so on and on and on. In all these forms of meditation is implied activity of thought, the activity of imitation, a movement of conformity, that is, an established order. And this is called meditation – including Zen. And to the speaker, this is not meditation at all.

Meditation is something entirely different. Meditation is to be aware of thought and feelings, never to correct, never to say it is right or wrong, never to justify, but just to watch and move with thoughts. In that watching, moving with thought and feeling, you begin to understand its whole movement.

Out of this awareness comes silence. Not stimulated or controlled silence, not silence put together by thought, which is stagnation, dead, but the silence that comes when thought has understood its own beginning, the nature of itself, how it is never free and always old. To see all the so-called meditations, to see how thought works, to see the movement of every conscious or unconscious thought, and in the understanding of it, which is to be aware of it, out of that comes silence. And this whole process is meditation, in which the observer never is.

Meditation is the quality of mind that is completely attentive and silent. Only then can you see a flower, the beauty of it, the colour of it, the shape of it, and only then does the distance between you and the flower cease.

To observe needs energy, the same energy that is now broken up into various activities. Attention is the focusing of all this energy, without fragmentation. When you so attend, that is, to observe, listen, watch, see, the mind must be very quiet, very still. It is only in that stillness you can really see or listen. The stillness of the mind is part of meditation. Stillness cannot be induced, cultivated or practised.

With this silence, the quietness of the mind, look at the responses, reactions, prejudices, fears, miseries, the quarrels – all the things that go on in life – so that the whole structure of existence, inwardly first, becomes somewhat clear, non-fragmented. Then any problems that arise – and there must be problems; you cannot avoid them – are understood immediately and resolved so that no energy is wasted. This can only be done when the mind is completely quiet inwardly. This is part of meditation.

The wider significance of meditation is to – not to

experience because there is no such thing as experiencing reality, enlightenment — but a mind so alert, so attentive in itself, it has a quality of timelessness, a quality not touched by thought. Thought always brings about fragmentation. There is in meditation a sense of spaceless ecstasy. And beyond this is something much more that cannot possibly be put into words. If it is put into words, it will not be the real thing. You cannot look for it; you can't go to a school to learn about it. By sitting day after day, you won't get it. But the question humanity has always been asking, seeking this strange unknown, to penetrate into that without the observer, to let that unknown penetrate itself, is meditation.

Part of meditation is to see the outer actually as it is, not as you wish it to be.

A meditative mind, having no concentration, has attention. Attention is entirely different from concentration. In concentration, there is the entity that concentrates on something, and so there is a duality. In concentration, there is resistance against intrusions of other movements. There is always a battle going on between wanting to concentrate on something and your thoughts wandering off. This conflict goes on throughout life.

You think you will be a marvellous meditator when you can completely control your thoughts. But thought when controlled withers, leads to illusion, hysteria and neurotic activity. Instead, see the quality of thought; understand that it can never be new, can never be free because it is born of the past, of experience and knowledge, which is of yesterday.

Attention is entirely different from concentration. In attention, there is neither the observer nor the observed, but only the state of attention from which things can be observed. Do this with me now, if you are at all serious and listening to what is being said with your heart and mind, with your sensitivity and affection, with your love and care. Listen to it, and you will see that in attention is the absence of any opinion or judgement, the absence of the observer. Therefore, in that attention, time is not.

There is the chronological time of yesterday, today and tomorrow. That is the movement of thought, which is time. In attention, in the quality of attention, there is only that state – oh, I don't know how to describe it! The description is not the described. But if you are attentive, you will know what it means. That attention is not to be practised. Don't go to schools to learn attention. Don't go to a guru and say, 'Please teach me what it is to be attentive.' When you ask another what it is to be attentive, you are not attentive. But to know that you are not attentive is attention.

From attention comes the quality of silence, a completely quiet mind. A mind that is completely quiet is free from the movement of the known. This quality of attention, with its astonishing silence, comes naturally when the mind understands all we have said.

Silence is not the space between two noises. Silence is not the product of thought desiring to be silent in order to achieve further experience. In silence, there is no experience. In silence, there is a totally different quality.

Any form of deliberate meditative practise is like any other form of desire.

Meditation covers the whole field of existence. Meditation implies freedom from methods or systems. I don't know what meditation is, so I start from there. Therefore I start with freedom, not with the burden of others.

In meditation there is no direction.

Sleep is as important as keeping awake, perhaps more so. If during the day the mind is watchful, self-recollected, observing the inward and outward movement of life, at night meditation comes as a benediction. The mind wakes up, and out of the depth of silence, there is the enchantment of meditation, which no imagination or flight of fancy can ever bring about. It happens without the mind inviting it: it comes into being out of the tranquillity of consciousness, not within it but outside of it, not in the periphery of thought but beyond its reaches.

There is no memory of meditation, for remembrance is always of the past, and meditation is not the resurrection of the past. It happens out of the fullness of the heart and not out of intellectual brightness and capacity. It may happen night after night, but each time, if you are so blessed, it is new. It is not new as in being different from the old, but new without the background of the old, new in its diversity and changeless change.

Sleep becomes a thing of extraordinary importance – not the sleep of exhaustion, not the sleep brought about through drugs or physical satisfaction, but a sleep that is as light and quick as the body is sensitive. And the body is made sensitive through alertness. Sometimes meditation is as light as a breeze that passes by; at other times its depth is beyond all measure. But if the mind holds one or the other as a remembrance to be indulged in, the ecstasy of meditation comes to an end. It is important never to possess or desire possession of it. The quality of possessiveness must never enter into meditation, for meditation has no root or any substance the mind can hold.

Meditation is not the repetition of mantras, not merely sitting down and breathing carefully. Meditation must be totally uninvited, not contrived, not put together. Which means there is no measurement.

Meditation has nothing to offer; you may not come begging with folded hands. It doesn't save you from any pain. It makes things abundantly clear and simple. But to perceive this simplicity, the mind must free itself, without any cause or motive, from all the things it has gathered through cause and motive. This is the whole issue in meditation.

Meditation is the purgation of the known. To pursue the known in different forms is a game of self-deception. Then the meditator is the master; there is not the simple act of meditation. The meditator can act only in the field of the known and must cease to act for the unknown to be. The unknowable does not invite you, and you cannot invite it. It comes and goes like the wind, and you cannot capture it and store it away for your benefit or use. It has no utilitarian value, but without it, life is measurelessly empty.

The question is not how to meditate, what system to follow, but what meditation is. The *how* can only produce what the method offers, but the very inquiry into what meditation is will open the door to meditation. The inquiry does not lie outside of the mind but within the movement of the mind itself.

In pursuing that inquiry, what becomes all-important is to understand the seeker and not what you seek. What you seek is the projection of your cravings, compulsions and desires. When this fact is seen, all searching ceases, which in itself is enormously significant. Then the mind is no longer grasping at something beyond itself. There is no outward movement with its reaction inwards. When seeking has entirely stopped, there is a movement of the mind that is neither outward nor inward. Seeking does not end by any act of will or by a complex process of conclusions. To stop seeking demands great understanding. The ending of search is the beginning of a still mind.

Meditation is not the repetition of words, sitting in a dark corner, looking at your own projections, images and ideas. Meditation is the unravelling of the known and freeing oneself from the known.

At all costs, avoid any system of meditation because a mechanical mind cannot possibly find out what truth is.

This is part of meditation: to free the mind from all pressure. This means no practice because practice is pressure.

Belief, imagination and faith have no place in meditation because belief, imagination and faith create illusion, a delusion in which the mind is caught.

Any form of conscious meditation is no meditation.

Meditation is the freeing of the mind of its content as consciousness that has created its own little space.

When the brain is completely quiet, it is empty. It is only through emptiness that anything can be perceived. You need space and emptiness to observe. To observe you, I must have space between you and me, and then there is seeing.

A mind crippled with sorrow and problems, with its vanities and the urge to fulfil, a mind that is frustrated and caught in nationalism – all the petty little things of life – such a mind has no space. It is not empty and therefore is utterly incapable of observing. When a shallow, petty mind says, 'I must explore something beyond,' it has no meaning. It must explore itself, not whether there is something beyond.

When the brain is completely quiet and empty – which demands astonishing awareness and attention – it is the beginning of meditation. Then it can see, listen, observe. Then it will find out if there is something beyond measure.

Meditation is the emptying of the content of consciousness.

Meditation is the emptying of the mind completely and totally. You cannot empty the mind forcibly, according to any method, system or school. You must see the utter fallacy of this. The pursuit of a system is the pursuit of experience, to achieve a further, or the ultimate, experience. When you understand the nature of experience, you brush all this aside with one sweep. It is finished forever, so that your mind never follows anybody, pursues no experience or visions. All visions, all heightened sensitivity is self-centred activity, either through drugs, discipline, rituals, worship or prayer.

Meditation is freeing the mind from the known.

A mind that has no space in daily life cannot possibly come upon that which is eternal, timeless. This is why meditation becomes extraordinarily important. Not the meditation that you practise, which is not meditation at all, but the meditation we are talking about that transforms the mind. It is only such a mind that is religious. Only such a religious mind can bring about a different culture, a different way of life, a different relationship, a sense of sacredness and therefore great beauty and honesty. All this comes naturally without effort, without a battle, without sacrifice, without control. And this is the beginning and the ending of meditation.

Meditation is to understand or come upon space that is not put together by thought, the 'me' and the 'not me'.

When you have space, the mind naturally becomes silent. This is important, not all the tricks we play upon ourselves to make the mind quiet, by repeating mantras, Transcendental Meditation, this, that or the other, that you call meditation. You can make your mind quiet by taking a pill, drugging yourself, taking a tranquiliser – the mind becomes very quiet. Whereas, when the mind has space, which means no direction, no operation of will and therefore no fear, there is silence. The mind is really quiet, not made quiet through tortuous means, but actual silence of which you are not aware. The moment you are aware that you are silent, it is not silence. Therefore meditation is part of the freedom from the experience of being silent.

Meditation takes place when you are not there.

Beauty is where you are not. The essence of beauty is the absence of the self. The question of meditation is having put the house in order, to meditate. The word *meditation* means to ponder over, to think over, to inquire into the abnegation of the self.

Where there is silence, there is space. Those of us who live in towns, in flats, in houses in narrow streets with noise, pollution of the air, earth and rivers, trees and nature, have very little space physically. When we have little space, we become violent, aggressive. When the mind has little space, it is in a constant state of revolt, a constant state of ugly discontent, wanting to express itself in violence, anger, brutality and various forms of aggression.

Where there is silence, there is space. There is no space if there is a centre. Where there is a centre as the 'me', the observer, the experiencer demanding more experience or wanting to get rid of experiences, there must be a diameter, a circle. You may extend or contract the circle, but the extension and the contraction are not space. Space only exists when the centre does not.

In that quietness, in that sense of beauty and love, there is quite a different kind of movement that is nameless, that cannot be described and can never be communicated to another. The mind must come upon it knowing itself, knowing all the tricks and cunningness, all the imaginings, all the trials and travails of life. Then, when it comes upon it, there it is. And that is the nature of a religious mind and meditation.

Meditation is something tremendously serious, not something that helps you relax, do better work or get more money. It is the total abnegation of the self.

What is meditation? It is a state of mind in which the operation and exercise of will are not. It has no direction. It is not seeking any experience. It is no longer seeking at all. Therefore a meditative mind is free of all control.

All our life, from childhood until we die, in pain, in strife, in anxiety, with a sense of loneliness, not knowing what love is, or wanting love, we are taught to control ourselves – control our anger, our ambition, our thoughts. We don't inquire into why we should control at all. And who is the controller? The controller is thought, the past that says to itself, 'This must not be, that must be. This must be suppressed, that must be pursued.'

In control there is imitation, conformity, suppression and the fear of not succeeding, not becoming, not achieving. To those people who call themselves religious, control means austerity. The word *austerity* means harsh, dry – a dry mind, a mind that has been controlled, is withered, brutalised, hurt. Such a mind can never know the austerity of simplicity, the austerity of love, the austerity of beauty. It will only know denial, harshness and the dry withering quality of control.

Meditation is not the withering of the mind that comes through control, suppression, conformity, through pursuing a pattern. You might ask, 'How is a mind that has no control to live in this world?' Perception and observation are greater than control. When you see something as false, that very perception brings about its own learning. That learning is non-control.

Freedom has its own order, which is not the order of control. Freedom has its own movement in bringing about order, in which so-called discipline is non-existent. Discipline means to learn. Not to conform, not to imitate, not to suppress, but to learn. Learning in itself brings order, without imposing an order from outside. A meditative mind has no control but is free. That freedom moves in order.

Let's find out what meditation is in order to go beyond. But first of all, let's find out what it is not. When you see the false as false, that is the truth. Do you see the beauty of this? When you see the truth in the false, that is the truth. When you lie, when you deceive, when you are dishonest or corrupt, see that, and that is the truth. So, in finding out what meditation is not, the false in meditation, we will know the truth of it. Through negation come to the positive, not the other way round.

Control in any form is not meditation. Control your thought, control your body, control your instincts — to control or suppress is not meditation. Control implies a controller. The controller is the one who says, 'I must shape my thought. I must suppress thoughts or pursue only one thought.' Where there is the division between the controller and the controlled, there must be conflict. Have you noticed, when you want to control, the conflicts you go through? And your tradition says you must control your thoughts, be the master of thought. But the master is another fragment of thought that has assumed authority over the other. Any form of control denies sensitivity, intelligence which is demanded in meditation.

Control is not in the movement of meditation, so we can completely put that aside. A method, a system or a practice are not meditation because they imply conformity to the pattern set by somebody who says they know what meditation is. When someone says they know what meditation is, they do not know. Beware of the one who says, 'I know' – they have lost all sense of humility and have ceased to learn. Enlightenment isn't a fixed end. It is a timeless movement in love.

A method, a system, a pattern, following, obedience, all imply conformity and a thing to be achieved as a fixed end, something permanent that is over there – which means time. Are enlightenment, wisdom and the clarity of truth a matter of time, or is it there for you to see? Your eyes are clouded when you are pursuing methods, systems and all the rest of the nonsense that goes on in the name of meditation all over the world.

Meditation is not control. Meditation is not a practice. Meditation is not the practise of attention or awareness.

There is something timeless beyond all thought and measure. We can call it, for the moment, truth. There is that truth that is sacred. Humanity has sought this thing but has been trapped by unnecessary things on its journey to find it.

To come to truth, you must have an extraordinarily quiet mind, free of all problems, a mind that has established right relationship with others, that in itself has complete, absolute order. We are using the word *absolute* in its real sense: an order that has no conflict, no contradiction in yourself, and from that, no fear, the understanding of pleasure and the ending of sorrow. When there is the ending of sorrow and fear, and the understanding of pleasure, out of that understanding comes love and compassion with its intelligence. When that is well-established, not verbally or intellectually but actually, meditation is that quality of mind that is wholly silent. In that silence, there is that which is eternal, which is sacred, beyond all images, all churches and all organisations.

Meditation implies freedom from measurement, that is, freedom from time.

Meditation is the transformation of the mind, a psychological revolution so that you live, in daily life, not in theory, not as an ideal, but in every movement of life, with compassion, love and the energy to transcend the pettiness and narrowness, the shallow life that you lead. When the mind is quiet, really still, not made still through desire or will, there is a totally different kind of movement that is not of time. To describe it would be absurd, just a verbal description, therefore not real.

What is important is the art of meditation. The word *art* means putting everything in its right place — not that which is contained in the museums but everything in our daily lives. That is the art of meditation, and in that there is no confusion. When there is order in your daily life, righteous behaviour and a mind that is completely quiet, the mind will find out for itself whether there is the immeasurable or not. Until you find that out, that which is the highest form of holiness, your life is dull, meaningless — as most people's lives are.

That is why meditation, right meditation, is absolutely necessary, so that the mind is made young, fresh, innocent. Innocence means a mind that is incapable of being hurt. All that is implied in meditation, which is not divorced from our daily living. In the very understanding of our daily living, meditation is necessary. That is, to attend completely to what you are doing. When you talk to somebody, the way you walk, the way you think, what you think, to give your attention to that. That is part of meditation.

Meditation is not an escape. It is not something mysterious. Out of meditation comes a life that is holy, a life that is sacred, and therefore you treat all things as sacred.

What is the origin of all our sorrows, all our suffering, the aching, the anxiety, our seeking security?

There is complete security in compassionate intelligence. Total security. But we want security in ideas, beliefs, concepts and ideals. We hold on to them, and that is our security, however false, however irrational it is. Where there is compassion, there is supreme intelligence and security. When you are compassionate, when there is that intelligence, there is no question of security.

There is an origin, the original ground from which all things start. That original ground is not the word; the word is never the thing. Meditation is to come upon that ground, the origin of all things that is free from all time. This is the way of meditation, and blessed is the one who finds it.

Meditation is the inquiry into that which is sacred.

Meditation is the beginning of order. Meditation is the awareness of the movement of thought as the 'me'. Meditation is freedom, the total, absolute inward freedom in which there isn't a single image – freedom from all the things that we have put together as reality: philosophically, psychologically, in other ways. When that takes place, the natural sequence is the flowering of silence.

In that silence is that quality of energy you have not touched before, and that is the transforming factor, the real creative movement of life. In that silence, there are a great many other things that go on because the mind as a whole, as well as the brain, becomes orderly. It will function when necessary; otherwise it is completely quiet. In this sense of silence, thought has no place. Therefore there is no time. That silence cannot be measured. If you are capable of measuring it, it is not silence but the silence thought has put together and therefore knows. Thought can measure it: 'I am silent today, I will be silent tomorrow.'

Meditation is a most extraordinary thing if you know what it is. In that quiet stillness, that which cannot be described, which is nameless, which is not the product of time and thought, there is that movement, and that is all there is. And that is the creation.

Sources

Learning about oneself is the beginning of meditation
Public Talk 8 in Paris, 21 September 1961

There is no meditation if there is no self-knowing
Public Talk 9 in Paris, 24 September 1961

*Meditation is to understand the whole movement of the
  known*
Public Talk 3 at Rajghat, 29 November 1981

If I am aware that I am neurotic
Public Talk 9 in Saanen, 1963

Investigating the ending of sorrow is part of meditation
Public Talk 5 in New Delhi, 24 December 1970

Self-knowledge is the beginning of meditation
Public Talk 8 in Paris, 21 September 1961

Meditation is the understanding of the self
Commentaries on Living Series III

In meditation, you must understand the significance of thought
Public Talk 4 in San Francisco, 25 March 1975

In meditation, don't follow anybody
Public Talk 4 in San Francisco, 25 March 1975

Our minds are trained to accept and conform
Public Talk 4 in Bangalore, 13 January 1974

If you are deeply interested in this question of meditation
Public Talk 4 in New York, 28 April 1974

Meditation is the denial, the negation of all systems
Public Talk 4 in New York, 28 April 1974

Authority and following another have no place
Public Talk 4 in Santa Monica, 24 March 1974

*Meditation is the discovery, the attention that brings order in
    your life*
Public Talk 6 In Madras, 26 December 1976

Is it possible for the mind to end conflict?
Discussion with Students in Schönried, 8 July 1969

Meditation is bringing about order in life
Public Talk 6 in Ojai, 18 April 1976

Real meditation is not possible if I don't understand conflict
Discussion with Students in Schönried, 8 July 1969

If you meditate without order
Public Talk 6 in Bombay, 7 February 1982

In the non-attentive state is conflict
Public Talk 3 in Madras, 13 January 1971

There is no controlling or disciplining thought
Public Talk 4 in San Francisco, 25 March 1975

When there is control, there is direction
Dialogue 18 with Allan W. Anderson in San Diego,
    California, 28 February 1974

Meditation in daily life is action
Public Talk 4 in New Delhi, 19 November 1972

Meditation is necessary for the mind to be completely still
Public Talk 4 in Bangalore, 13 January 1974

Any form of control denies sensitivity
Public Talk 4 in New Delhi, 19 November 1972

What is meditation?
Commentaries on Living Series II

The mind is an instrument
Commentaries on Living Series II

There is security in total intelligence
Public Talk 4 in New Delhi, 19 November 1972

In total silence there is nothing
Public Talk 4 in Ojai, 20 April 1975

Meditation is to have a completely still mind
Public Talk 4 in Ojai, 20 April 1975

Silence cannot come through practice or control
Public Talk 6 in Madras, 8 January 1978

The brain has its own rhythm
Public Talk 6 in Bombay, 7 February 1982

Meditation without a set formula
Krishnamurti's Notebook

A man was sitting cross-legged
The Only Revolution

Meditation is not the repetition of words
The Only Revolution

Can the mind be absolutely still?
Public Talk 4 in San Francisco, 25 March 1975

Meditation demands tremendous attention
Public Talk 4 in Bangalore, 13 January 1974

Meditation is total attention to whatever you are doing
Public Talk 2 in New York, 28 March 1982

The word 'meditation' is very loaded
Public Talk 10 in Saanen, 30 July 1967

Meditation is not the repetition of words
Public Talk 8 in Madras, 17 December 1961

At all costs, avoid any system of meditation
Public Talk 3 in Madras, 13 January 1971

This is part of meditation
Public Talk 1 in Madras, 24 December 1977

Belief, imagination and faith have no place
Public Talk 4 in New York, 28 April 1974

Any form of conscious meditation is no meditation
Discussion 3 with Teachers at Brockwood Park, 23
    September 1984

Meditation is the freeing of the mind
Dialogue 18 with Allan W. Anderson in San Diego, 28
    February 1974

When the brain is completely quiet
Public Talk 10 in Saanen, 28 July 1963

Meditation is the emptying of the content of consciousness
Public Talk 6 in Ojai, 18 April 1976

Meditation is the emptying of the mind completely
Public Talk 9 in Saanen, 30 July 1964

There is something timeless beyond all thought and measure
Interview by Gary Null at Brockwood Park, 17 October
    1980

Meditation implies freedom from measurement
Public Talk 4 in San Francisco, 25 March 1975

Meditation is the transformation of the mind
Public Talk 4 in San Francisco, 25 March 1975

What is the origin of all our sorrows
Public Talk 4 in New Delhi, 8 November 1981

Meditation is the inquiry into that which is sacred
Public Talk 4 In Madras, 15 December 1974

Meditation is the beginning of order
Public Talk 4 in New Delhi, 2 December 1973

ABOUT THE AUTHOR

Krishnamurti spoke not as a guru but as a friend, and his talks and discussions are based not on tradition-based knowledge but on his own insights into the human mind and his vision of the sacred. He left a large body of literature in the form of public talks, writings, discussions with teachers and students, scientists and religious figures, conversations with individuals, television and radio interviews and letters. Many of these have been published as books, and audio and video recordings.

For more information, please visit kfoundation.org.